New Jersey

THE GARDEN STATE

by Eric Siegfried Holtz

Curriculum Consultant: Jean Craven,
Director of Instructional Support,
Albuquerque, NM, Public Schools

WORLD ALMANAC® LIBRARY

Please visit our web site at: **www.worldalmanaclibrary.com**
For a free color catalog describing World Almanac® Library's
list of high-quality books and multimedia programs, call
1-800-848-2928 (USA) or 1-800-387-3178 (Canada).
World Almanac® Library's fax: (414) 332-3567.

Library of Congress Cataloging-in-Publication Data

Holtz, Eric Siegfried.
    New Jersey, the Garden State / by Eric Siegfried Holtz.
        p. cm. — (World Almanac Library of the states)
    Includes bibliographical references and index.
    Summary: Illustrations and text present the history, geography, people, politics
and government, economy, and social life and customs of New Jersey, the home
of Thomas Edison's laboratory and the Campbell Soup Company.
    ISBN 0-8368-5141-2 (lib. bdg.)
    ISBN 0-8368-5311-3 (softcover)
    1. New Jersey—Juvenile literature. [1. New Jersey.] I. Title. II. Series.
F134.3.H65   2002
974.9—dc21   2002066815

This edition first published in 2002 by
World Almanac® Library
330 West Olive Street, Suite 100
Milwaukee, WI 53212 USA

Design and Editorial: Bill SMITH STUDIO Inc.
Editor: Kristen Behrens
Assistant Editor: Megan Elias
Art Director: Olga Lamm
Photo Research: Sean Livingstone
World Almanac® Library Project Editor: Patricia Lantier
World Almanac® Library Editors: Monica Rausch, Mary Dykstra, Jacqueline Laks Gorman,
 Jim Mezzanotte
World Almanac® Library Production: Scott M. Krall, Tammy Gruenewald,
 Katherine A. Goedheer

Photo credits: pp. 4-5 © Eyewire; p. 6 (bottom) © Corel; (top right) © Corel; (bottom right)
© PhotoDisc; p. 7 (top) © PhotoDisc; (bottom) Campbell's Soup Company; p. 9 © Corel;
p. 10 © Dover; p. 11 © Library of Congress; p. 12 © Library of Congress; p. 13 © Library of
Congress; p. 14 © CORBIS; p. 15 © PAINET INC.; p. 17 © Library of Congress; p. 18 © Adam
Giuliano/NewarkNJ.info; p. 19 © Ray Stubblebine/Reuters/TimePix; p. 20 (left to right) Atlantic
City CVB; © PAINET INC.; Atlantic City CVB; p. 21 (left to right) © PAINET INC.; © Corel;
© Corel; p. 23 David Muench/CORBIS; p. 26 (top) © PhotoDisc; (bottom) © Library of Congress;
p. 27 courtesy of Johnson & Johnson; p. 29 © Joseph Sohm/CORBIS; p. 31 (all) © Library
of Congress; p. 32 © Library of Congress; p. 33 © Lee Snider; Lee Snider/CORBIS; p. 34
© Library of Congress; p. 35 (top) © Kevin Winter/DMI/TimePix; (bottom) © Dover; p. 36
© Ray Stubblebine/Reuters/TimePix; p. 37 © Gary Hershorn/TimePix; p. 38 © ArtToday; p. 39
© PhotoDisc; p. 40 © John Dominis/TimePix; p. 41 © PhotoDisc; pp. 42-43 © Library of
Congress; p. 44 (top) © PhotoDisc; (bottom) © Corel; p. 45 (top) © PhotoDisc; (bottom) © Corel

Printed in the United States of America

1 2 3 4 5 6 7 8 9 06 05 04 03 02

New Jersey

The New Jersey Dynamo

New Jersey is one of the busiest places in the United States. The Dutch, the first Europeans to settle the area, came with business on their minds, hoping to make their fortunes. During the Revolutionary War, New Jersey was the site of many battles, including the pivotal Battle of Trenton, which helped end the war and make the United States a reality.

New Jersey grew and prospered as immigrants arrived and established themselves in many lines of work. At the beginning of the twentieth century, Thomas Alva Edison, called the "top most significant man of the millennium" by *Life* magazine, set up a laboratory in Menlo Park and busied himself with inventions that would help make the modern world.

Today the state's big businesses keep millions of people at work producing goods that are shipped around the world. The Port of New Jersey bustles, while farms in the southern part of the state produce gorgeous flowers that find their way into homes nationwide.

Well-known New Jerseyans include political leaders such as Thomas Paine, who lived in Bordentown and whose stirring words helped give birth to a nation. Centuries later, Bill Bradley leaped to fame as a professional basketball player and then tackled national issues as a U.S. senator from New Jersey. Anne Morrow Lindbergh, also from New Jersey, became famous for both her pioneering feats as an aviator and her thoughtful prose. Buzz Aldrin, from Montclair, went even further than other local heroes when he became the second man to walk on the Moon in 1969.

A bridge in the capital city of Trenton bears the proud slogan "Trenton Makes — The World Takes." It is a statement that could be made about the state as a whole, as New Jersey has stayed busy over the years producing leaders, artists, dreamers, and achievers whom the world has welcomed with open arms.

▶ Map of New Jersey showing the interstate highway system, as well as major cities and waterways.

▼ A sandy pathway among the dunes leads to one of New Jersey's Atlantic beaches.

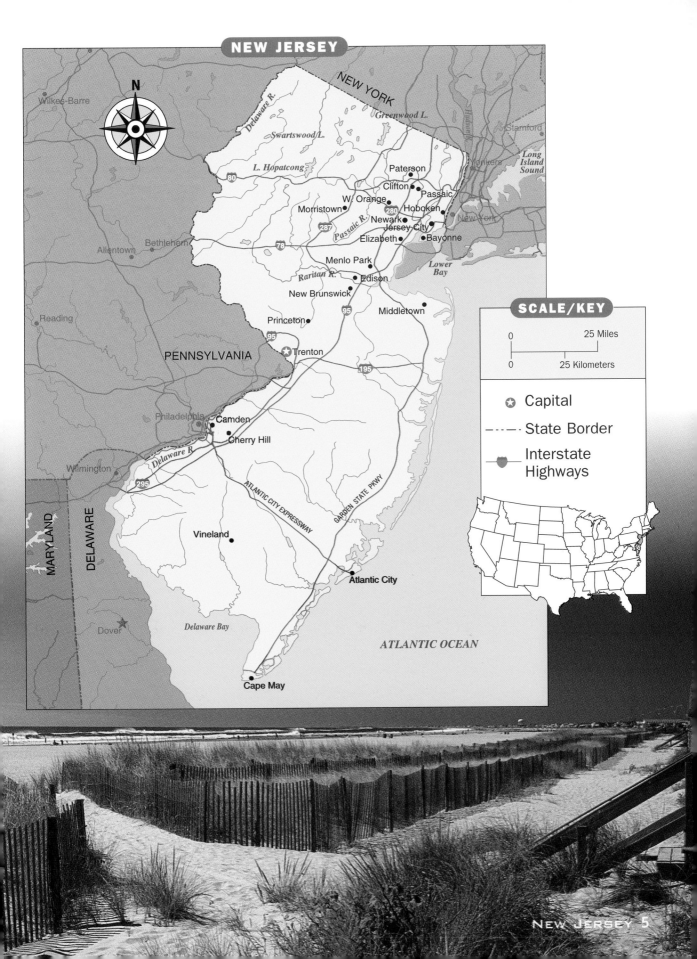

NEW YORK

Wilkes-Barre

Delaware R.

Greenwood L.

Stamford

Swartswood L.

Yonkers

Long Island Sound

L. Hopatcong

80

Paterson

Clifton

Passaic

New York

W. Orange

Hoboken

Morristown

280

Newark

Jersey City

Allentown

Bethlehem

287

Passaic R.

Elizabeth

Bayonne

78

Menlo Park

Lower Bay

Raritan R.

Edison

New Brunswick

Reading

95

Middletown

Princeton

PENNSYLVANIA

95

Trenton

195

Philadelphia

Camden

Cherry Hill

Wilmington

Delaware R.

295

ATLANTIC CITY EXPRESSWAY

GARDEN STATE PKWY

MARYLAND

DELAWARE

Vineland

Atlantic City

Dover

Delaware Bay

ATLANTIC OCEAN

Cape May

Fast Facts

NEW JERSEY (NJ), The Garden State

Entered Union
December 18, 1787 (3rd state)

Capital	Population
Trenton	85,403

Total Population (2000)
8,414,350 (9th most populous state) — *Between 1990 and 2000 the population of New Jersey increased 8.9 percent.*

Largest Cities	Population
Newark	273,546
Jersey City	240,055
Paterson	149,222
Elizabeth	120,568

Land Area
7,417 square miles (19,210 square kilometers) (46th largest state)

State Motto
"Liberty and Prosperity"

State Song (Unofficial)
"I'm From New Jersey,"
by Red Mascara, adopted in 1935

State Bird
Eastern goldfinch

State Animal
Horse — *The U.S. Equestrian (horseback-riding) Team has its headquarters in Gladstone.*

State Insect
Honeybee

State Fish
Brook trout

State Flower
Purple violet — *Violets are not only pretty to look at, they taste great, too. You can find violet-flavored candies, chocolate, and even ice cream.*

State Seashell
Knobbed whelk — *Commonly known as the conch, this mollusk can be found all along New Jersey's Atlantic coast. It is sometimes harvested for food.*

State Dinosaur
Hadrosaurus foulkii — *A nearly complete fossilized skeleton of this creature was found in Haddonfield in 1858. The discovery changed science by proving that dinosaurs really existed.*

State Tree
Red oak — *The acorns from this tree were once an important source of food for Native Americans who inhabited the area.*

State Dance
Square dance

PLACES TO VISIT

Historic Speedwell, *Morristown*
Alfred Vail and Samuel Morse invented the telegraph here. Their invention began the communications revolution that continues to this day with E-mail and the Internet.

Space Farms Zoo & Museum, *Beemerville*
This institution began in 1927 as an animal shelter. It now encompasses 100 acres (40 hectares) and houses the largest collection of exotic animals in the United States.

Museum of American Glass, Wheaton Village, *Millville*
More than 6,500 pieces of American glass are on display. Glass-blowing and manufacturing demonstrations are also featured.

For other places and events, see p. 44.

For other places and events, see p. 44.

BIGGEST, BEST, AND MOST

- Goliath, the largest bear ever measured, lived in New Jersey. He was 12 feet (4 meters) tall and weighed about 2,000 pounds (908 kilograms).
- Northlandz in Flemington claims to have the most extensive miniature railway in the world. It includes 8 miles (13 km) of track.
- New Jersey farms produce two-thirds of the world's eggplants.
- The IMAX Dome Theater at the Liberty Science Center in Jersey City is the largest in the United States.

STATE FIRSTS

- **1811** The first ferry service in the United States began between Hoboken and Manhattan, New York.
- **1878** John Holland of Passaic County built the first practical submarine. It is now on display at the Paterson Museum.
- **1933** The first "drive-in" movie theater was built in Camden County.

The Jersey Devil

The tale of the Jersey Devil is one of the nation's most enduring myths. It dates to the 1700s when Daniel and Jane Leeds learned they were expecting their thirteenth child. The prospect of having yet another child was so daunting that Jane Leeds is supposed to have said, "I wish this child be born a devil." According to some accounts she got her wish. There have been reports ever since of a strange creature in the Pine Barrens of New Jersey. It mostly looks like a huge flying lizard with the head of a horse. Sometimes, though, it looks like a hairy man with red eyes and horns. New Jersey's professional hockey team, the New Jersey Devils, is named for this legend.

Mmm, Mmm, Good

The Campbell Soup Company was formed in Camden in 1869. Joseph Campbell was a fruit merchant who teamed up with Abraham Anderson, an icebox manufacturer, to sell canned vegetables. The company's breakthrough came in 1897 when Dr. John T. Dorrance invented condensed soup. Condensing the soup, or removing water from it, made it cheaper to package, store, and transport. Campbell's Soup has since become one of the nation's best-known convenience foods. Campbell's Soup is now sold all around the world and includes some varieties you won't find in the United States — such as Watercress and Duck-Gizzard Soup, which is sold in China.

The Pathway State

This is a very good Land to fall with, and a pleasant Land to see.
— *Robert Juet, logbook of the* Half Moon, *1609*

The first people to live in what is now New Jersey arrived about ten thousand years ago. These small groups of nomadic hunter-gatherers gradually developed semipermanent settlements and farming methods. The Late Woodland period in New Jersey (A.D. 500 to A.D. 1638) was dominated by a group called the Lenni-Lenape. In their Algonquian language, *Lenni-Lenape* means "original people." The Europeans called them the Delaware.

Relations between European settlers and Native people in New Jersey were relatively peaceful in comparison to most other European colonies. Foreign diseases nevertheless took a heavy toll on the Native American population. By the early 1800s, as white settlements continued to grow, the Lenni-Lenape were pushed out of New Jersey completely. Today their descendants live primarily in Canada and Oklahoma.

European Exploration and Settlement

In 1497, Italian Giovanni Caboto, better known as John Cabot, may have been the first European to see the New Jersey coast as he explored the coast of North America for England's King Henry VII. Like Christopher Columbus before him, Cabot was looking for a western route to Asia. Giovanni da Verrazano, another Italian, who was exploring North America for the French, explored New Jersey's coast more thoroughly in 1524. It was not until 1609, however, that a European is known to have set foot in New Jersey.

Englishman Henry Hudson, in command of the Dutch ship the *Half Moon,* sailed into New York Bay and up what came to be called the Hudson River, exploring the surrounding land in New York and New Jersey as far as present-day Albany, New York. Not long after, the Dutch West India Company established settlements in the region,

---

Native Americans of New Jersey
Subgroups of the Lenni-Lenape:

Minsi (northern New Jersey)

Unami (southern New Jersey)

Unilachtigo (southern New Jersey)

DID YOU KNOW?

New Jersey is named after Jersey, one of the Channel Islands between England and France. One of New Jersey's original proprietors, Sir George Carteret, was born there.

which came to be called New Netherland. The Dutch established the first permanent settlement in present-day New Jersey at Bergen, which is now Jersey City, in 1660. At that time the Dutch colony claimed all the land from the mouth of the Connecticut River to Burlington Island on the Delaware River, including Manhattan Island.

Unlike settlers elsewhere — such as those of the Massachusetts Bay Colony — settlers in New Netherland had not come to escape religious or political persecution. The Dutch came to the colony in hopes of making their fortunes, in particular from the plentiful supply of fur. Swedish settlers also trickled into what is now southern New Jersey, calling their colony New Sweden. New Sweden lasted from 1638 until 1655, when the Dutch took it over. The English were even more forceful. The Dutch surrendered all of New Netherland to the English in 1664.

The New Jersey Colony

After claiming New Netherland in England's name, King Charles II of England granted the territory to his brother, James. James assigned it to Lord John Berkeley and Sir George Carteret, two proprietors (owners) who renamed it New Jersey. Berkeley and Carteret sold parcels of land at very reasonable prices and also permitted settlers of all political and religious persuasions to settle in the territory. This made New Jersey an attractive destination for people who wanted to escape from social and religious restrictions in Europe.

▼ During the colonial era, settlers established small farms like the one portrayed here in New Jerseyan Jasper Cropsey's *Jersey Meadowlands*.

In 1673, Berkeley sold his portion of New Jersey to a group of English Quakers, religious dissenters who were not welcomed in many of the other colonies. In 1676, New Jersey was divided into two colonies, East Jersey and West Jersey, the latter a Quaker colony. When Carteret died, another group of Quakers bought East Jersey and settled there.

Settlers in East and West Jersey became angry that they had to pay rent to the colony's owners rather than being allowed to purchase land. Their anger sparked rebellion, and in 1702 all of New Jersey became a colony of the British crown, administered by the governor of New York. The colony was once again united as New Jersey, but it maintained two capitals. Perth Amboy was the capital of the east and Burlington was the capital of the west.

For more than thirty years, New Jersey was governed by the New York governor. New Jerseyans were not happy with this state of affairs and, in 1738, they were finally given their own governor. Lewis Morris was governor of the province of New Jersey from 1738 until 1746.

Revolution

Resistance to colonial government hardened after the French and Indian War (1754–1763). The British had spent a great deal of money fighting that war and wanted their American colonies to pay more taxes to make up for it. Many colonists objected to "taxation without representation." In 1774, a group of New Jerseyans — inspired by the famous Boston Tea Party — burned a shipment of tea in Greenwich. Two years later, at the Continental Congress in Philadelphia, Pennsylvania, New Jersey declared itself independent of British rule, on July 2, 1776. The colony's delegates soon also signed the Declaration of Independence.

While battling the British, New Jerseyans also fought among themselves. Those who took the side of the British were called Loyalists or Tories,

▼ This 1851 painting of General George Washington and his troops crossing the Delaware River, by Emanuel Leutze, is historically inaccurate — the boat is the wrong type and the flag portrayed was not used for another six months. Still, it has become one of the most recognized depictions of the Revolutionary War.

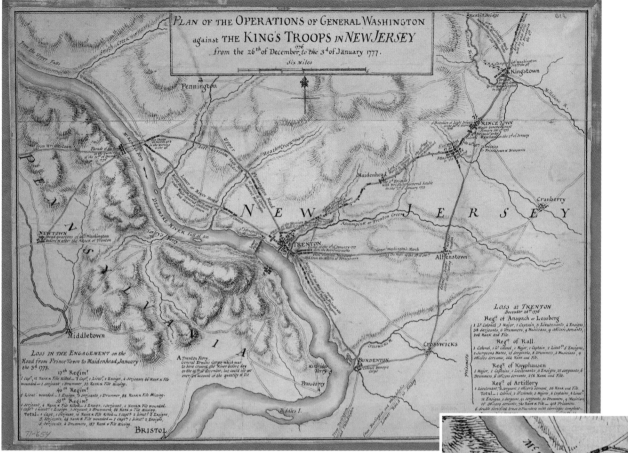

PLAN OF THE OPERATIONS OF GENERAL WASHINGTON against THE KING'S TROOPS IN NEW JERSEY from the 26th of December, to the 3d of January 1777.

▲ This 1777 map shows the British army's version of battles with George Washington's troops between December 26, 1776, and January 3, 1777.

while rebelling colonists called themselves Patriots. Some of the most important battles of the Revolutionary War were fought in New Jersey. They included the Battle of Trenton, where George Washington's army secretly crossed the Delaware River to defeat the British on December 26, 1776. This was soon followed by another U.S. victory at the Battle of Princeton. Washington's army then spent the winter in Morristown. In June 1778 the Battle of Monmouth ended in a draw. At this battle Mary Hays, who was the wife of an American soldier, carried pitchers of cold water to thirsty fighting men, earning her the nickname Molly Pitcher. The last major battle in New Jersey was the Battle of Springfield, where the British were defeated in June 1780.

Princeton served as the nation's temporary capital from June to November 1783. Then, Trenton became the capital in December 1784. Trenton even came close to becoming the permanent capital of the United States, but lost out to Washington, D.C. New Jersey also had an important role in framing the new U.S. Constitution. Delegates from New Jersey proposed a senate with equal representation from all states, thus guaranteeing small states like New Jersey a strong voice in government. Satisfied with this assurance, New Jersey became the third state to ratify the Constitution, on December 18, 1787.

Early Statehood

The first New Jersey state constitution of 1776 limited the power of the governor by allowing more people to vote. Anyone with a certain amount of property who had lived in the state for a certain amount of time could vote. The wording in the constitution did not specify that property owners had to be men or that they had to be white, although this is undoubtedly what the authors intended to say. Women of property and free African-American men took advantage of this loophole and voted in elections until 1807, when the constitution was rewritten to exclude them.

In 1790, New Jersey unified its state capital at Trenton. The state's population and economy grew rapidly throughout the 1800s, especially in the northeast. New Jersey became one of the great centers of the Industrial Revolution, which had begun to transform the world. Even more famously, New Jersey developed state-of-the-art road, rail, and canal links with New York and Pennsylvania. With industrialization came great wealth but also some side effects, including a growing gap between rich and poor.

The Civil War

Although it had abolished slavery between 1804 and 1846 and some residents maintained "stations" for the Underground Railroad, New Jersey was not ardently antislavery. In both 1860 and 1864, New Jersey was one of the very few free states not carried by Abraham Lincoln, the Republican party presidential candidate opposed to the spread of slavery. New Jersey violently resisted the military draft. In 1863, New York City draft riots spread to Newark, and several African Americans were killed. Nevertheless, the state made great sacrifices for the Northern victory in the Civil War. About 88,000 New Jerseyans fought and about 6,300 died. In contrast to the Revolutionary War, when approximately one hundred battles were fought in the state, no battles took place in New Jersey during the Civil War.

▼ This Civil War recruiting poster was published in February 1865.

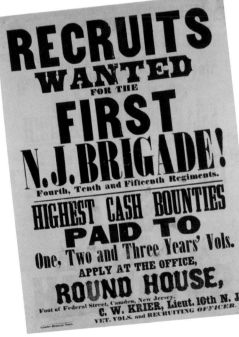

Industrialization

The Civil War accelerated New Jersey's industrialization. People moved from the countryside into the cities in a trend known as urbanization. By the late 1800s, New Jersey was on its way to becoming one of the most urbanized states in the nation. Huge numbers of immigrants arrived from other countries, especially Germany, Italy, Ireland, and Eastern Europe. By 1910, half of the state's population was made up of immigrants or the children of immigrants. Many immigrants streamed into the country via New York's Ellis Island.

New Jersey had an abundant labor supply. Its transportation facilities were the most advanced in the world. It was right in the middle of the booming markets of the northeast. Its corporate regulations were also very relaxed. This attracted some of the nation's leading companies and made New Jersey an industrial powerhouse. Meanwhile the New Jersey government derived high revenues from the fees these companies paid to incorporate within the state.

The state's success, however, came with a reputation as the "mother of trusts." Trusts, also called monopolies, were huge companies that often controlled entire industries. New Jersey had more trusts than any other state. Many people thought that trusts were unfair to competitors, customers, and employees. They were also considered to have a corrupting influence on government and society as a whole. As public opinion turned against the trusts, pressure grew on New Jersey to control them.

Woodrow Wilson, a New Jersey governor (and later U.S. president), is credited with taming the trusts. He proposed a series of laws that were passed by the state legislature in 1913. The laws came to be known as the

Thomas Alva Edison

Thomas Edison (1847–1931) was one of the world's greatest inventors. He is credited with an amazing range of inventions and received more than one thousand patents. Many of his breakthroughs were made in his laboratories at Menlo Park and West Orange. Edison's first patent was for an electric vote recorder intended to speed up the process of counting votes. When the Massachusetts legislature refused to buy it because they were not interested in making their election process more efficient, Edison swore never again to invent something that people did not want. Among the most familiar of his inventions are the light bulb, the phonograph, and the motion picture camera. He also greatly improved existing technologies, including the electric battery, the telegraph, and the telephone. Edison was noted for his methodical approach to inventing.

Seven Sisters Acts. The "Sisters" were seven large corporations, including the giant Standard Oil, that controlled coal, oil, steel, railroads, and other businesses.

This legislation attempted to "level the playing field" by limiting the size of corporations. The acts were successful, but they were repealed in the same year they were passed. Despite their short life, the acts were considered landmarks of the Progressive Era, a period in U.S. history during which many people advocated social and political reforms. Progressive Era reforms in New Jersey included establishing worker's compensation and municipal utilities, and replacing mayors with commissions in some city governments.

Early Twentieth Century

New Jersey's vast industrial capacity meant that it was an important producer of arms and supplies during the two World Wars. In the years between the wars, the market for arms dried up, and in the Great Depression of the 1930s, worldwide demand for other products collapsed as well. At the height of the Depression, huge numbers of New Jerseyans were out of work. The government programs known as the New Deal helped keep some people working. Many were employed by the government to build public

▲ This 1889 political cartoon by Joseph Keppler illustrates the power of trusts. The large men in the back row watch to make sure the senators (seated at desks) enact laws that ensure the trusts grow ever fatter. Among the trusts pictured are steel, coal, and Standard Oil.

DID YOU KNOW?

All of the street names used on the board game Monopoly are from Atlantic City except for Marvin Gardens, which was taken from Marven Gardens in nearby Margate City and accidentally misspelled.

works projects, such as roads. The Depression, however, did not really end until the United States geared up for World War II, and demand increased for manufactured goods.

In 1937, a famous disaster occurred in New Jersey. The *Hindenburg*, which was the largest and fastest dirigible (blimp) ever built, crossed the Atlantic and crashed as it was landing in Lakehurst. Thirty-five people were killed and the event ended the era of passenger travel in airships.

Late Twentieth Century and Present Day

The early postwar years were prosperous, but worrying trends were under way. Many industries moved out of the cities and into the suburbs, along with much of the middle-class population. The big cities — with fewer jobs and decreased tax revenues to pay for government services — were increasingly left to poorer people. Conditions in the cities deteriorated through the 1960s until riots broke out in 1967 in Newark and in Trenton in 1968. Since then, efforts have been made to provide more services to the inner cities, but progress has been uneven.

Industrialization brought economic benefit to New Jersey but also caused serious environmental damage. After years of minimal regulation, strict laws and regulations were put in place to reduce pollution and repair past damage. Modern New Jersey is working both to maintain its industrial base and protect its environment.

New Jersey has long been among the wealthiest states in the nation, at the cutting-edge of modern trends. New Jersey continues to prosper, and today, as it was more than two hundred years ago, it is still a major destination for immigrants from around the world. The difficulties New Jersey has faced have made the state stronger and ready to meet new challenges.

Ellis Island, New Jersey!

Between 1892 and 1924, more than 12 million immigrants from around the world passed through Ellis Island (*below*) on their way into the United States. Almost 40 percent of U.S. citizens can trace their ancestry through the island's registry room. Most people believed that the whole of Ellis Island was part of New York State. It turns out that only 3.3 acres (1.3 ha) encompassed by the original boundaries of the island belong to New York. Over the years the island was built out with landfill and greatly expanded. Those additions — some 90 percent of the island — are legally part of New Jersey. Ellis Island is now part of the Statue of Liberty National Monument, controlled by the federal government.

A Concentrated State

> That noe person qualified as aforesaid within the said Province at any time shalbe any waies molested punished disquieted or called in Question for any difference in opinion or practice in matters of Religious concernements.
>
> — *Concessions and Agreements of the Proprietors, 1665*

New Jersey is the nation's fifth smallest state, but it has the ninth largest population. With 1,134.5 people per square mile (438 people per sq km), it is the most densely populated state. It is also an extremely urban state, second only to California, with 89 percent of the population living in towns and cities. Seventy-five percent of the population lives within 30 miles (48 km) of New York City.

Since so many people live close to New York, the whole region is sometimes considered one big city — a megalopolis with a population of more than twenty-one million. Separately, however, Newark is the state's largest city, followed by Jersey City, Paterson, and Elizabeth. All are in the northeastern area of the state. Another 15 percent of the state's population lives in central New Jersey, around the

Age Distribution in New Jersey
(2000 Census)

Age	Population
0–4	563,785
5–19	1,720,322
20–24	480,079
25–44	2,624,146
45–64	1,912,882
65 & over	1,113,136

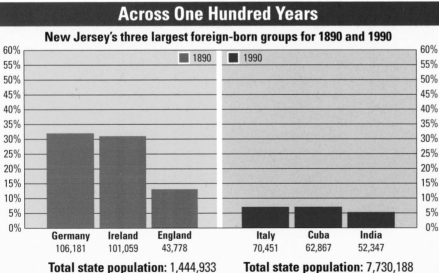

Across One Hundred Years

New Jersey's three largest foreign-born groups for 1890 and 1990

■ 1890 ■ 1990

	1890			1990		
	Germany	Ireland	England	Italy	Cuba	India
	106,181	101,059	43,778	70,451	62,867	52,347

Total state population: 1,444,933
Total foreign-born: 328,975 (23%)

Total state population: 7,730,188
Total foreign-born: 966,610 (13%)

Patterns of Immigration

The total number of people who immigrated to New Jersey in 1998 was 35,091. Of that number, the largest immigrant groups were from India (12.2%), the Dominican Republic (7.1%), and Peru (5.8%).

capital, Trenton, and Camden. During the summer months the populations of towns along the shore and in the country expand, as urban dwellers escape from the heat.

Immigration

New Jersey's population has risen rapidly throughout its modern history. That pattern continues today with an 8.9 percent increase in residents between 1990 and 2000. Much of that increase has come from waves of immigration. In the seventeenth century the Dutch and Swedish were the first Europeans to settle in the area, followed by the English, Irish, Scottish, Welsh, French, and Belgians in the early eighteenth century. Huge numbers of Germans, Italians, and Hungarians poured into New Jersey thereafter.

▲ New Jerseyans have always enjoyed the combination of urban life and oceanside or rural relaxation that their state provides. This photograph of residents and visitors at the Bradley Bathing Pavilion in Asbury Park was taken in 1902.

Heritage and Background, New Jersey — Year 2000

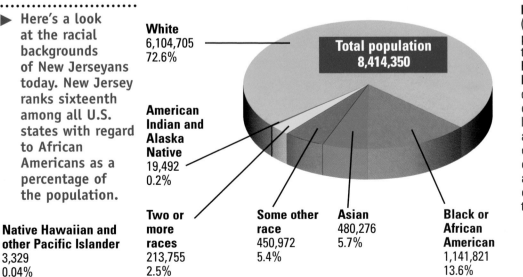

► Here's a look at the racial backgrounds of New Jerseyans today. New Jersey ranks sixteenth among all U.S. states with regard to African Americans as a percentage of the population.

Note: 13.3% (1,117,191) of the population identify themselves as **Hispanic** or **Latino,** a cultural designation that crosses racial lines. Hispanics and Latinos are counted in this category as well as the racial category of their choice.

White
6,104,705
72.6%

**Total population
8,414,350**

American Indian and Alaska Native
19,492
0.2%

Native Hawaiian and other Pacific Islander
3,329
0.04%

Two or more races
213,755
2.5%

Some other race
450,972
5.4%

Asian
480,276
5.7%

Black or African American
1,141,821
13.6%

African Americans have lived in the state from around the beginning of the era of European settlement, but after the Civil War the African-American population expanded significantly as many left the South to seek opportunities elsewhere. Hispanics — especially Puerto Ricans, Mexicans, and Cubans — arrived in large numbers during the second half of the twentieth century. Their numbers continue to increase rapidly. Asians are also a fast-growing minority, especially Indians, Chinese, Filipinos, and Koreans. The face of New Jersey is ever-changing. The state's median age of 36.7 is close to the national median of 35.3.

Religion

Most New Jerseyans — approximately 85 percent — are Christians. Roman Catholics, the largest Christian group, make up about 42 percent of all New Jersey residents. Baptists (10 percent), Methodists (7 percent), and

Educational Levels of New Jersey Workers (age 25 and over)	
Less than 9th grade	486,210
9th to 12th grade, no diploma	718,996
High school graduate, including equivalency	1,606,555
Some college, no degree or associate degree	1,070,455
Bachelor's degree	826,887
Graduate or professional degree	457,130

▼ The skyline of Newark, New Jersey's most populous city.

Lutherans (3 percent) are three other large Christian communities in the state. New Jersey's Jewish population has been a significant presence in the state since 1698, when Aaron Louzada, a Sephardic Jew, settled his family in Bound Brook. Today, 6 percent of the state's population is Jewish. This percentage is higher than the national average of 2.7 percent. Approximately 0.6 percent of the population is Muslim, 0.3 is Hindu, and 0.6 agnostic (people who neither believe nor disbelieve in God).

Education

Public education was not common anywhere in the world until the nineteenth century. Before 1871, when the Free School Law was passed in New Jersey, most students had to pay a fee to attend public schools. In 1836, Newark became the site of the state's first public high school, although only boys could attend. Recently, New Jersey made a major investment in education. The state spends considerably more per pupil than the national average.

Some of the country's oldest and most prestigious universities are found in New Jersey. There are more than thirty public institutions in the state, most notably Rutgers, The State University of New Jersey. It was established in New Brunswick as Queen's College in 1766. The New Jersey Agricultural Experiment Station is part of Rutgers. Other branches of Rutgers are in Camden and Newark.

Of the state's twenty-five four-year private institutions of higher education, Princeton University is the oldest and best known. It was founded in 1746 as the College of New Jersey. Princeton's highly distinguished departments include the Woodrow Wilson School of Public and International Affairs. The Institute for Advanced Study and the Princeton Theological Seminary are also located at Princeton.

▲ The parking lot at Giants Stadium in the Meadowlands was not filled with football fans on September 16, 2001. Instead, volunteers gathered to organize goods donated by the New Jersey Sports and Exhibition Authority. Supplies were then trucked into New York City and distributed to rescue workers and other volunteers searching through the debris at "Ground Zero" — the site of the World Trade Center, which had been destroyed by a terrorist attack five days before.

From Sea to Mountains

> . . . which said tract of land is hereafter to be called
> by the name or names of New Caeserea or New Jersey.
>
> — *Land Grant to Lord John Berkeley and Sir George Carteret, 1664*

While some parts of New Jersey are highly industrialized and densely populated, much of the state is largely unspoiled with a relatively small population. The New Jersey Pinelands National Reserve in the southeast occupies more than 1.1 million acres (445,170 ha), or about 23 percent of the state. Because of the environmental damage the state has suffered, New Jersey now has some of the strictest environmental laws in the nation.

Plains

About three-fifths of New Jersey, in the south, is part of the Atlantic Coastal Plain, where elevations do not rise above 100 feet (30 m). Much of this area has fertile, loamy soil. It is populated mostly with resort towns, the most famous being Atlantic City. Farther inland is a lush area called the Greensand Belt, which has given New Jersey its nickname, the Garden State. This is the state's richest agricultural area.

Highest Point

High Point
1,803 feet (550 m)
above sea level

▼ *From left to right:*
Canada geese sail New Jersey's coastal marshland; a swamp rose grows in the Brigantine National Wildlife Refuge; a marina outside Atlantic City; Cape May beaches, which front the Atlantic Ocean and are a popular summer destination; a New Jersey farm; the Delaware River in autumn.

Mountains and Valleys

The state's highest mountains are found in northwestern New Jersey in an area called the Appalachian Ridge and Valley. This region includes the state's highest point, which is located in the Kittatinny Mountains at a spot aptly called High Point. It is 1,803 feet (550 m) above sea level. The Appalachian Valley on the eastern side of the Kittatinny Mountains is the center of the state's dairy industry. Southeast of this area lies the Piedmont Plateau.

Rivers and Lakes

New Jersey is largely bordered by water. Most of eastern New Jersey is part of the Atlantic coastline. What remains of eastern New Jersey is bordered by the Hudson River, which forms the northeastern border with New York. The Delaware River separates the state from Pennsylvania to the west and Delaware to the south. These rivers are of great economic importance to the state and the entire region. Vast amounts of trade and industry follow the rivers down to their ocean outlets. The longest river belonging entirely to New Jersey is the Raritan River in the north of the state. It is about 75 miles (121 km) long. Most of New Jersey's roughly eight hundred lakes and ponds lie in the north. The largest is Lake Hopatcong.

Climate

New Jersey is known for its highly seasonal climate. Summers are hot and humid, while winters are cold and snowy. The change of seasons is unmistakable. Autumn foliage colors are especially spectacular. Weather conditions are less extreme along the coast, where ocean

Average January temperature
Newark: 31°F (-0.6°C)
Atlantic City: 31°F (-0.6°C)

Average July temperature
Newark: 77°F (25°C)
Atlantic City: 75°F (24°C)

Average yearly rainfall
Newark: 43 inches (109 cm)
Atlantic City: 41 inches (104 cm)

Average yearly snowfall
Newark: 28 inches (71 cm)
Atlantic City: 16 inches (41 cm)

Major Rivers

Delaware River
390 miles (628 km)

Hudson River
306 miles (492 km)

Passaic River
80 miles (129 km)

Raritan River
75 miles (121 km)

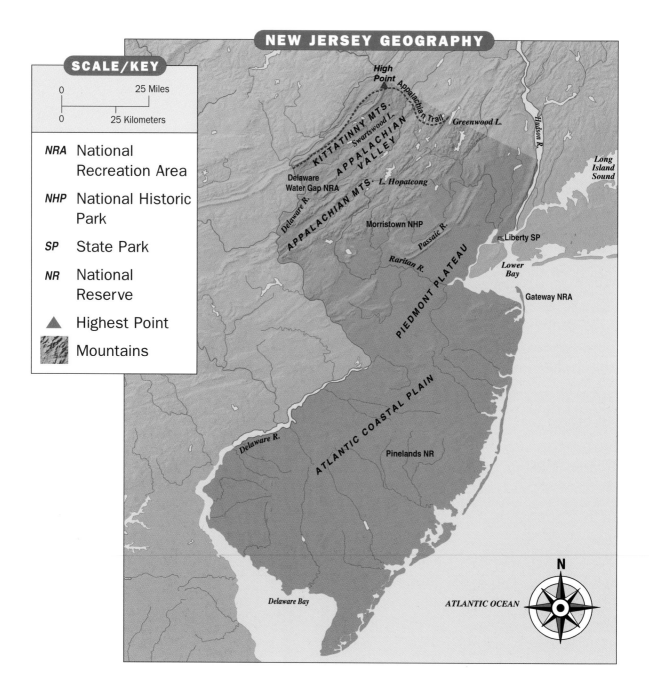

NEW JERSEY GEOGRAPHY

SCALE/KEY

0 — 25 Miles
0 — 25 Kilometers

NRA — National Recreation Area
NHP — National Historic Park
SP — State Park
NR — National Reserve
▲ — Highest Point
Mountains

High Point
Appalachian Trail
KITTATINNY MTS.
Swartswood L.
APPALACHIAN VALLEY
Greenwood L.
Hudson R.
Long Island Sound
Delaware Water Gap NRA
L. Hopatcong
APPALACHIAN MTS.
Delaware R.
Morristown NHP
Passaic R.
PIEDMONT PLATEAU
Liberty SP
Raritan R.
Lower Bay
Gateway NRA
ATLANTIC COASTAL PLAIN
Delaware R.
Pinelands NR
Delaware Bay
ATLANTIC OCEAN
N

Largest Lakes

Lake Hopatcong
2,686 acres
(1,087 ha)

Greenwood Lake
1,920 acres
(778 ha)

Swartswood Lake
504 acres
(204 ha)

breezes take the edge off both summer and winter, but blizzards and hurricanes are not unknown there.

Plants and Animals

Forests cover more than 40 percent of New Jersey. The coastal plain forests are dominated by pine, oak, and cedar. Northern forests are typically a mix of oak, maple, birch, hickory, and hemlock. The violet, the state flower, is common throughout the state. Other flowers include honeysuckle, goldenrod, azalea, and rhododendron. The state has a thriving cultivated plant and flower industry.

Strict conservation measures have renewed the state's wildlife populations, which had been threatened by uncontrolled industrial and residential growth. Black bears can once again be found in the northern forests and have become so accustomed to humans that they sometimes wander through suburban areas. Deer and coyotes are expanding their range throughout the state, sometimes posing a threat to other animals or humans. New Jersey also has its share of smaller creatures such as chipmunks, skunks, squirrels, frogs, and turtles. Many bird species live in the state throughout the year. Many more make seasonal stopovers as they migrate along the route known as the Atlantic Flyway. The flyway is also used by monarch butterflies, which go south for winter. The New Jersey coast is also famous for its shellfish, part of a diverse marine ecosystem and extensive fishing industry.

A Unique Environment

The New Jersey Pine Barrens are a sprawling ecosystem in the southeastern part of the state that take their name from their vast forest (12,000 acres or 4,860 ha) of rare, pygmy oaks and pines. The trees are less than 12 feet (4 m) tall. While parts of the Pine Barrens are marshy, others are very dry. Frequent fires and sandy soil in the dry areas both have caused trees to remain small. The wetlands are home to many rare plant species, including a type of orchid that only grows in the Pine Barrens and in South Africa.

Garden of Industry

> Genius is one per cent inspiration,
> ninety-nine per cent perspiration.
> — *Thomas Alva Edison, U.S. inventor, circa 1903*

For such a small area, New Jersey has natural resources that are surprisingly extensive. Even more impressive, however, are New Jersey's industrial might and inventiveness. While the nickname Garden State is not misplaced, industry has really set New Jersey apart.

Historically, manufacturing has played a significant part in the state's economy, becoming the leading industry by 1900. The state was at the forefront of the Industrial Revolution. New Jersey was home to laboratories for Thomas Edison, Bell Labs, Albert Einstein, and many others. Their discoveries did much to advance modern technology. The electric light, the communications satellite, and the transistor at the heart of electronics were all invented or improved in New Jersey. That may be one reason why services — including knowledge-based industries — have today supplanted manufacturing as the most valuable economic sector within the state.

Agriculture and Fisheries

New Jersey's more than 9,600 farms cover about one-fifth of the state, and more than one hundred types of produce are cultivated. Of all the state's agricultural products, flowers (especially roses), ornamental shrubs and other plants, and sod from New Jersey's many greenhouses, nurseries, and sod farms produce the most income. Dairy products, livestock, tomatoes, peaches, and apples are also important to New Jersey's economy. The state also ranks high in the production of cranberries and blueberries. Fisheries along the Atlantic Coast yield a varied harvest, the most noteworthy items being clams and other shellfish.

Top Employers (of workers age sixteen and over)
Services 33.2%
Wholesale and retail trade 20.6%
Manufacturing . . 16.9%
Finance, insurance, and real estate 8.9%
Transportation, communications, and other public utilities 8.6%
Construction 6.0%
Public Administration . . . 4.7%
Agriculture, forestry, and fisheries 1.0%
Mining 0.1%

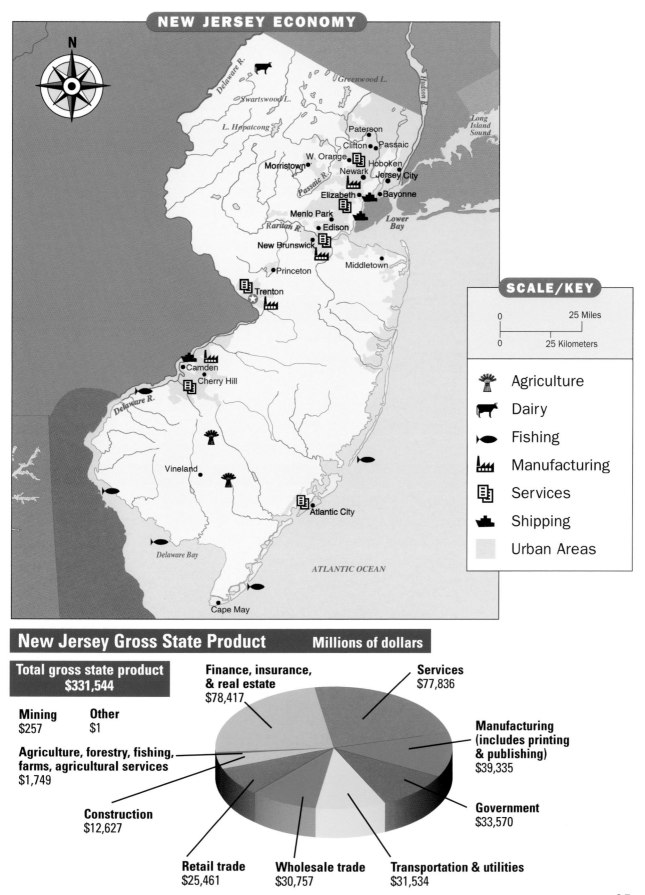

NEW JERSEY ECONOMY

SCALE/KEY

0 — 25 Miles
0 — 25 Kilometers

🌾 Agriculture
🐄 Dairy
🐟 Fishing
🏭 Manufacturing
🏢 Services
🚢 Shipping
⬜ Urban Areas

New Jersey Gross State Product
Millions of dollars

Total gross state product
$331,544

Finance, insurance, & real estate
$78,417

Services
$77,836

Mining
$257

Other
$1

Manufacturing (includes printing & publishing)
$39,335

Agriculture, forestry, fishing, farms, agricultural services
$1,749

Government
$33,570

Construction
$12,627

Retail trade
$25,461

Wholesale trade
$30,757

Transportation & utilities
$31,534

Manufacturing

New Jersey is one of the nation's leading manufacturing states. Chemicals are the most important of New Jersey's manufactured products, with pharmaceuticals being the most valuable category of chemicals. Johnson & Johnson and Merck are two major pharmaceutical companies headquartered in New Jersey. Printing and publishing are the next most profitable manufacturing activities. Food processing, which includes canned foods such as Campbell's Soup, comes next. Electrical equipment, fabricated metal products, and scientific instruments are also important manufactured products. The Newark-Jersey City-Elizabeth area in the northeast and the Trenton-Camden area in west-central New Jersey are the main manufacturing zones.

Forestry and Mining

New Jersey's forest industries are not extensive. One of the leading activities is the growing of Christmas trees — close to 600,000 are harvested each year. Granite and basalt are the state's leading mining products, followed by sand, gravel, peat, and clay.

Transportation

Because New Jersey is located in the middle of the United States's busy Northeast Corridor, it became a transportation hub early in the 1900s. The state's road, rail, air, and water transportation are today among the most sophisticated in the world. The corridor between New

Made in New Jersey

Leading farm products and crops
Flowers
Milk
Tomatoes
Peaches
Apples
Cranberries
Blueberries

Other products
Chemicals
Printing and publishing
Processed food
Electrical equipment

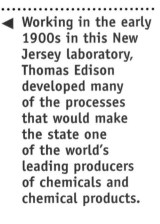

◄ Working in the early 1900s in this New Jersey laboratory, Thomas Edison developed many of the processes that would make the state one of the world's leading producers of chemicals and chemical products.

York City and Philadelphia is particularly well served by road and rail. Many New Jerseyans commute daily to jobs in those cities. The area's transportation system is so tightly integrated that many facilities are run by the Port Authority of New York and New Jersey, a joint commission created in 1921.

There are more than 35,000 miles (56,315 km) of public highways in the state, including the New Jersey Turnpike. Railroad tracks total 912 miles (1,467 km). Newark International Airport is one of the nation's busiest. The seaports of Newark-Elizabeth, regulated by the Port Authority of New York and New Jersey, are among the most important in the nation. Smaller ports lie on the Delaware River at Paulsboro, Camden, Gloucester City, and Trenton. The state is a leader in containerized port facilities, which are seamlessly integrated with road and rail networks.

▲ Johnson & Johnson employee Earle Dickson invented the first adhesive bandage in 1920. Today, more than eighty years later, Band-Aids™ have generated more than $100 billion in sales worldwide.

Services

New Jersey's service industries are its fastest-growing economic sector, with finance, insurance, and real estate the leading categories in this sector. Large insurance companies, including Prudential, are based in the state. Community, business, and personal services are next, followed by wholesale and retail trade. The services sector also includes fields like management, computer programming, health care, hospitality, communications, education, and tourism.

Tourism generates about $20 billion per year in revenues. Tourists are mostly attracted to the beaches along the Atlantic shore. Despite its famous boardwalk and Miss America Pageant, Atlantic City was fading as a tourist destination until gambling was legalized in 1978. The Appalachian and Pineland areas are other major tourist draws in New Jersey.

DID YOU KNOW?

The cranberry, grown in New Jersey, is one of three cultivated fruits native to North America. The others are the blueberry, also grown in New Jersey, and the Concord grape.

Major Airports		
Airport	Location	Passengers per year (2000)
Newark International	Newark	34,188,468
Atlantic City International	Atlantic City	907,108

Executive State

> That itt shall not be lawfull for the Governor of the said Province his heires or Sucsessors for the time being and Counsell or any of them at any time or times hereafter to make or enact any law or lawes for the said Province without the Consent act and Concurrance of the Generall Assembly.
>
> — *The Fundamental Agreements of 1681*

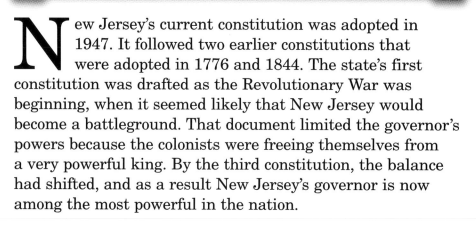

N ew Jersey's current constitution was adopted in 1947. It followed two earlier constitutions that were adopted in 1776 and 1844. The state's first constitution was drafted as the Revolutionary War was beginning, when it seemed likely that New Jersey would become a battleground. That document limited the governor's powers because the colonists were freeing themselves from a very powerful king. By the third constitution, the balance had shifted, and as a result New Jersey's governor is now among the most powerful in the nation.

The Executive Branch

The governor is the state's chief executive. He or she is elected for a four-year term and cannot serve more than two terms in a row. After a term out of office, however, a governor may serve again. The governor is the only elected executive official. Most others are appointed by the governor, with the approval of the state senate. The governor has the right to veto proposed legislation. The legislature can override the governor's veto with a two-thirds majority in both houses.

The Legislative Branch

The New Jersey State Legislature is composed of a senate and a general assembly. There are forty legislative districts in the state. Each district elects one senator and two assembly members. Senate terms run in cycles of two and

Four Governors in Eight Days

During an eight-day period in January 2002, a total of four different individuals held the title of Governor of New Jersey. In February 2001, Governor Christine Todd Whitman resigned her office to become the Environmental Protection Agency administrator for President George W. Bush. Following state law, the president of New Jersey's senate, Donald DiFrancesco, then became governor. But on January 6, 2002, the old senate was dissolved and the new senate was split 50-50, requiring a pair of co-presidents. The two senators agreed to share power, each spending three days in a row as governor. Then, on January 15, newly elected governor Jim McGreevy finally took office.

Elected Post in the Executive Branch		
Office	Length of Term	Term Limits
Governor	4 years	2 consecutive terms

four years. The two-year term is for the first election of a new decade, following a U.S. Census. Assembly members are elected to two-year terms. The legislature meets on even-numbered years on the second Tuesday of January. After two years any business not completed expires. Special sessions can also be called by the governor or a majority petition of both houses of the Legislature.

The Judicial Branch

New Jersey's judicial branch has three main divisions: the supreme court, the superior court, and the tax court. At the local level are municipal courts, part of the state's city governments. Civil, criminal, and family cases are tried in the superior court. Criminal cases arise when a person is accused of a serious crime. In civil cases one party claims that another party caused him or her harm. Family cases have to do with domestic situations. A decision can be appealed if either side believes the decision was unfair. The appellate division of the superior court (separate

▼ The New Jersey state capitol was built in 1792. Despite extensive renovations and a fire that destroyed much of the building in 1885, there are a few rooms from that original building still in use, including the governor's private chambers.

from the trial courts) hears appeals. If either party believes that a decision of the appellate division was wrong, that party can ask the state supreme court to hear the case. The tax court reviews actions of local tax boards and the state tax division. Municipal courts hear cases involving minor criminal offenses and disputes.

Most of the state's judges are nominated by the governor and approved by the state senate. Judges serve an initial seven-year term, after which they may be renominated and approved for a term that lasts until they reach age seventy. Municipal court judges are appointed by local governments and serve three-year terms. They can be reappointed for additional three-year terms. There are six associate justices and one chief justice on the New Jersey Supreme Court. The superior court has thirty-two judges in the appellate division and approximately 360 trial judges. There are twelve judges on the tax court.

Local Government

There are 588 municipalities in New Jersey, including villages, towns, townships, boroughs, and cities. They are usually governed by charters granted by the state and run by one of several systems, including mayors, council-managers, or commissions. County governments are called Boards of Chosen Freeholders because originally only property owners, or "freeholders," could serve on the boards. There are twenty-one boards in New Jersey. Each is responsible for maintaining local roads and bridges and a variety of other facilities. Each board has between three and nine members who are elected for three-year terms.

National Representation

Like the rest of the states, New Jersey has two senators in the U.S. Senate. The state also has thirteen representatives in the U.S. House of Representatives and fifteen Electoral College votes.

State Legislature			
House	**Number of Members**	**Length of Term**	**Term Limits***
Senate	40 senators	2 or 4 years	None
General Assembly	80 representatives	2 years	None

* For legislators taking office after 1992, there is a lifetime limit of four terms in the General Assembly and two in the Senate.

The White House via New Jersey

GROVER CLEVELAND
(1885–1889 and 1893–1897)

Although born in Caldwell, Stephen Grover Cleveland (1837–1908) was raised in western New York. His political career began when he was elected assistant district attorney of Buffalo, New York, in 1863. He was later elected governor of New York. A Democrat, Cleveland was elected president in 1884. He ran for re-election four years later. In that election Cleveland won the popular vote but did not win a majority of the Electoral College votes and was thus defeated. He ran again in 1892 and won. An economic depression made him unpopular, however, and his own party nominated another candidate for the next election. He is the only president to have served two nonconsecutive terms.

WOODROW WILSON (1913–1921)

Thomas Woodrow Wilson (1856–1924) was born in Staunton, Virginia, but entered politics while living in New Jersey. He began his public career as president of Princeton University. Local Democratic bosses encouraged him to run for governor of New Jersey in 1910, hoping they could control him. He proved them wrong, asserting his independence and stressing individual rights and social progressivism. While governor, he successfully ran for president in 1912. In his first term, measures were taken to break up the massive companies known as trusts. During his second term, the United States was drawn into World War I, and Wilson became a major figure on the world stage. He helped negotiate peace and establish the League of Nations, an early version of the United Nations.

New Jersey Politics

During the twentieth century, governorships in New Jersey have been roughly split between Democrats and Republicans. After a period of solid Republican majorities in the early twentieth century, control of the Legislature has lately shifted back and forth between the two major parties. Since 1900, New Jersey voters have tended to favor Republican candidates in presidential elections. A notable exception to this pattern came when the state's voters supported Democrat Franklin Roosevelt four times. They also voted Democratic in the elections of 1960 and 1964 and helped elect Bill Clinton, a Democrat, in 1992 and 1996.

DID YOU KNOW?

Frank Hague was known as "the Boss" long before Bruce Springsteen. Mayor of Jersey City for thirty years, Hague once declared, "I am the law!"

Beyond the Turnpike

> Camden [New Jersey] was originally an accident, but I shall never be sorry I was left over in Camden. It has brought me blessed returns.
>
> — *Walt Whitman, U.S. poet, 1880s*

New Jersey packs both a diverse population and a diverse landscape into a small area. From the Jersey Shore to the Appalachians, you can find a little of nearly everything. New Jersey has earned a reputation for practicality, and its citizens are known as hard workers, but there is more to the state than that. It has also been highly creative in finding ways to "work smarter." The available educational opportunities have reinforced that creativity. New Jersey has been second to none in the practical arts, but other arts — music, dance, theater, fine art, and architecture — also thrive in the state. What's more, outdoor and indoor leisure activities abound. Name a sport, and chances are that you will find the perfect place to play and watch it somewhere in the state.

Libraries and Museums

New Jersey's first public library was established in Trenton by Thomas Cadwalader in 1750. Now there are more than four hundred public library systems. Many libraries belong to the New Jersey Library Network, which pools the resources of member libraries for interlibrary loans. On average, each state resident accesses about six books per year from public libraries. Among the many historic sites

▼ The Chancellor Green Library, completed in 1873, was Princeton University's first full-service library.

in the state are George Washington's Revolutionary War headquarters in Morristown, Thomas Paines's home in Bordentown, and the Walt Whitman House in Camden.

The New Jersey State Museum in Trenton specializes in natural history, archaeology, and decorative and fine arts. Its facilities include a planetarium. The Newark Museum also includes a planetarium, with art, science, and natural history exhibits as well as a "mini-zoo" among its other attractions. Especially noteworthy is its collection of African and Tibetan art. Also in Newark is the New Jersey Historical Society Museum, dedicated to the history of the city, state, and region. In Jersey City, the Liberty Science Center celebrates the state's many great inventors and inventions. The leading museums dedicated to fine art are the Princeton University Art Museum; the Montclair Art Museum, which has an impressive collection of American and Native American art; and the Jane Voorhees Zimmerli Art Museum at Rutgers University in New Brunswick.

▲ The Liberty Science Center is just a ferry ride away from Ellis Island and the Statue of Liberty. The center's Experiment Gallery includes a demonstration of the principles Thomas Edison worked with when he invented the lightbulb.

Communications

The northeastern United States is one of the most concentrated media markets in the world. Information flows through the region with little respect for state lines. New Jersey has more than two hundred newspapers, about twenty of which are published daily. In 1777 the *New Jersey Gazette,* published in Burlington, became the state's first weekly newspaper. The *Newark Daily Advertiser,* founded in 1832, was the state's first daily newspaper. The leading

DID YOU KNOW?

Telstar 1 was the first satellite to transmit television live across the Atlantic Ocean. Launched in 1962, it was designed at Bell Laboratories in New Jersey.

dailies are now the *Star-Ledger* of Newark, the *Jersey Journal* of Jersey City, the *Record* of Bergen County, and the *Times* and the *Trentonian* of Trenton. Many New York City and Philadelphia publications are also widely read in New Jersey.

New Jersey has ten television stations and more than eighty radio stations. WJZ, established in Newark in 1921, was the state's first commercial radio station and only the second one licensed in the nation. WATV, the state's first television station, also began in Newark. It went on the air in 1948. Both WJZ and WATV are now based in New York.

Theater and Music

A recent addition to New Jersey's cultural life is the New Jersey Performing Arts Center, which opened in Newark in 1997. It is the nation's sixth-largest performing arts center, hosting many of the world's top musicians and dancers. The McCarter Theatre Center for the Performing Arts in Princeton received the 1994 Tony Award for Outstanding Regional Theater. Other notable theaters include the Paper Mill Playhouse in Millburn, the John Harms Center for the Arts in Englewood, the Trenton War Memorial Auditorium in Trenton (home of the New Jersey Symphony Orchestra), the South Jersey Regional Theater in Somers Point, and the State Theatre in New Brunswick. Community theaters are also an important part of the state's culture. Actors and entertainers from New Jersey include Jason Alexander, David Copperfield, Danny DeVito, Michael Douglas, Janeane Garofalo, Jerry Lewis, Ray Liotta, Bebe Neuwirth, Jack Nicholson, Joe Pesci, Kevin Spacey, Meryl Streep, and John Travolta.

◀ A 1939 Works Progress Administration (WPA) poster announces an exhibit at the Montclair Museum.

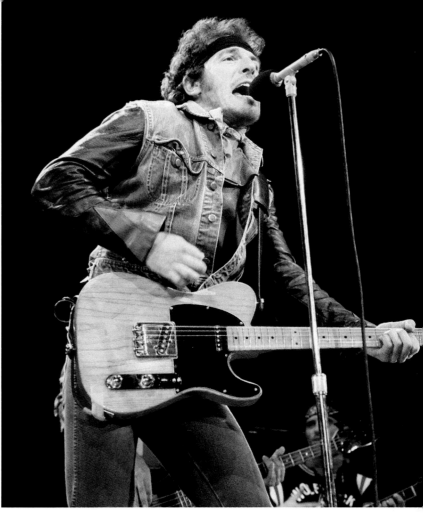

▶ "The Boss," Bruce Springsteen, on his 1984–1985 *Born in the U.S.A.* tour.

The New Jersey Ballet is one of the state's famous dance companies. Classical, jazz, and folk music festivals are held around the state, most famously in Cape May. Many popular musical performers come from New Jersey, including legends like Count Basie, Paul Robeson, Frank Sinatra, and Sarah Vaughan. More recently the state has given us Bruce Springsteen, Jon Bon Jovi, Whitney Houston, Lauryn Hill, and Ice-T. One of the region's main concert stages is Giants Stadium in the Meadowlands Sports Complex. The Meadowlands is a stopover for music superstars from around the world. The Blockbuster Sony Music Entertainment Center in Jersey City and the PNC Bank Arts Center in Holmdel are other major concert venues.

Important writers from New Jersey include children's book authors Judy Blume and Edward Stratemeyer; novelists James Fenimore Cooper, Stephen Crane, Norman Mailer, and Philip Roth; and poets William Carlos Williams, Allen Ginsberg, and Joyce Kilmer.

The Great Outdoors

Name an outdoor sport and there is a place to do it in New Jersey. From Asbury Park to Cape May, surfers ride the waves off the shore of Monmouth County. Some of the best breaks can be found near Seven Presidents Oceanfront Park in Long Branch, so named because for several decades it was the nation's "summer capital for U.S. presidents." President Ulysses Grant's 1869 summer sojourn started a trend that was followed by Presidents Rutherford B. Hayes, James Garfield, Chester Arthur, Benjamin Harrison, William McKinley, and Woodrow Wilson.

DID YOU KNOW?

Walt Whitman lived in Camden from 1873 until his death in 1892. Whitman's most famous book of poetry is *Leaves of Grass*.

Beach fun is not the only fun to be found in the state. In northern New Jersey hikers enjoy the wilderness along more than 70 miles (113 km) of the Appalachian Trail. Sailing, biking, swimming, fishing, and canoeing opportunities can be found from High Point State Park in the north to the Pine Barrens in the south.

For golfing enthusiasts there is the state golf course, Spring Meadow, in Farmingdale, in addition to more than 130 other public and private courses. One of the nation's best is at the Sand Barrens Golf Club in Swainton. The United States Golf Association Museum and Library can be found in Far Hills.

In winter months state parks also provide opportunities for ice fishing, snowmobiling, and cross-country skiing. Downhill skiers race down slopes at New Jersey's four ski resorts, which include Mountain Creek and Hidden Valley.

Sports

New Jersey is the home base of the U.S. Equestrian Team. It is also home to some of the nation's leading horse racetracks — the Meadowlands, Monmouth Park, and Freehold Raceway. The Meadowlands hosts the Hambletonian, one of harness racing's premier events. The entire Meadowlands Sports Complex in East Rutherford is a major sports venue. It includes an outdoor stadium and an indoor arena in addition to its racetrack. The Meadowlands is home to many of New Jersey's professional sports teams:

Sport	Team	Home
Basketball	New Jersey Nets	Continental Airlines Arena East Rutherford
Hockey	New Jersey Devils	Continental Airlines Arena East Rutherford
Soccer	NY/NJ MetroStars	Continental Airlines Arena East Rutherford

the New Jersey Nets of the National Basketball Association (NBA), the New Jersey Devils of the National Hockey League (NHL), and the NY/NJ MetroStars, a professional soccer team. Two National Football League (NFL) teams officially from New York — the New York Giants and New York Jets — play their home games in Giants Stadium at the Meadowlands.

The New Jersey Nets began play in 1967 as the New Jersey Americans in the American Basketball Association (ABA). The owners had hoped to find a permanent home in New York City but ended up in Teaneck. During the 1968–69 season, the team moved to Commack, New York, and changed its name to the New York Nets. They were a New York team until the 1975–76 season. The Nets became an NBA team when the ABA and the NBA merged in 1976, and they moved back to New Jersey after their first season in the NBA. Notable Nets include Julius "Dr. J." Erving, Kenny Anderson, and Jason Kidd. In 2002, the Nets made their first trip to the NBA championship finals. They were beaten by the Los Angeles Lakers, who took the title for the third time in a row.

The Nets's arena-mates, the New Jersey Devils, were originally known as the Colorado Rockies. The franchise was bought in 1982 by Dr. John McMullen, who moved the team to New Jersey, renaming them the Devils. In 1995 and 2000 the Devils won the NHL's Stanley Cup.

The NY/NJ MetroStars, a Major League Soccer team, has made it to the playoffs four times in their first six seasons.

◀ Kenyon Marton of the New Jersey Nets takes the ball past Chris Webber of the Sacramento Kings.

Jerseyans and Jerseyites

Say to the world that New Jersey
shares in the spirit of this age.
— *Robert Ingersoll, U.S. orator, 1887*

Following are only a few of the thousands of people who were born, died, or spent much of their lives
in New Jersey and made extraordinary contributions to the state and the nation.

AARON BURR

POLITICAL LEADER

BORN: *February 6, 1756, Newark*
DIED: *September 14, 1836, Port Richmond, NY*

Aaron Burr served in the Continental Army during the Revolutionary War. After the war, he practiced law in New York. In 1800, the Republican party nominated Thomas Jefferson for U.S. president and Burr for vice president. The Republican party received the most electoral votes, but the electors did not specify whether Jefferson or Burr should be president. Although he had stood as the candidate for vice president, Burr refused to let Jefferson assume the presidency. The matter went before

the House of Representatives, which finally chose Jefferson as president, angering Burr. While he was vice president, Burr ran for governor of New York. Alexander Hamilton opposed his candidacy, calling him "the most dangerous man in America." On July 11, 1804, the two fought a duel in Weehawken; Hamilton was killed. Burr became a fugitive but still served out his term as vice president. Burr then went west, where he conspired to found an empire. He was tried for treason, but Supreme Court Justice John Marshall, an enemy of Jefferson's, helped to acquit him. He returned to New York, where he practiced law until his death.

ALBERT EINSTEIN
SCIENTIST

BORN: *March 14, 1879, Ulm, Germany*
DIED: *April 18, 1955, Princeton*

Albert Einstein spent most of his boyhood in Munich, then moved with his family to Italy when he was fifteen. He went to Switzerland to study physics and math. He earned a diploma from the Swiss Federal Polytechnic School in 1901 and went to work for the Swiss Patent Office in 1902, pursuing his own research in his spare time. During this time, he formulated his revolutionary theory of relativity, which would change the way scientists thought about time and space. His research attracted attention, and Einstein received government and university appointments in Switzerland, Czechoslovakia, and Germany. He won the Nobel Prize for physics in 1921. Einstein had become a German citizen in 1914, but he renounced his citizenship and moved to the United States in 1933 when the Nazi regime came to power. He became a professor of theoretical physics at Princeton University, retiring in 1945. In his later years, he pursued his interest in the World Government Movement and helped establish Hebrew University in Jerusalem.

DOROTHEA LANGE
PHOTOGRAPHER

BORN: *May 26, 1895, Hoboken*
DIED: *October 11, 1965, San Francisco, CA*

Dorothea Lange was one of the great twentieth-century photographers. She contracted polio as a young girl, which left her with a limp and perhaps a greater sensitivity to human suffering. After studying photography in New York, she traveled and then moved to California. Her most famous photos were taken when she worked for the Works Progress Administration (WPA), one of U.S. president Franklin Roosevelt's New Deal programs. She took pictures of people desperately trying to survive both the Great Depression and the Dust Bowl of the 1930s. In 1941, she was awarded a Guggenheim Fellowship for her "photographic study of the American social scene." After World War II, she traveled, photographed, and exhibited her work around the world.

PAUL ROBESON
SINGER AND ACTOR

BORN: *April 9, 1898, Princeton*
DIED: *January 23, 1976, Philadelphia, PA*

Paul Leroy Bustill Robeson was the son of a former slave who escaped to become a minister in Princeton. Robeson won a scholarship to Rutgers University, where he excelled in sports, academics, theater, and music. While attending Columbia Law School, Robeson won acclaim as an actor. His legal career was short-lived, but his acting and singing careers flourished. In 1925, he delivered the first concert of spirituals by an African-American soloist. His most famous role was in the musical *Show Boat* (1928), where he sang the classic "Ol' Man River." His portrayal of Shakespeare's Othello is also legendary. Robeson encountered severe racism in his career, which increased his commitment to civil rights and led him to embrace communist beliefs. As a result, he became controversial and had difficulty finding work.

COUNT BASIE
MUSICIAN

BORN: *August 21, 1904, Red Bank*
DIED: *April 26, 1984, Hollywood, FL*

William Basie's mother gave him music lessons when he was a child. Basie began playing professionally as the piano accompaniment to vaudeville shows. In 1927, he started playing piano with a Kansas City, Missouri, band, and in 1935 he got the chance to lead his own band there. A radio announcer nicknamed him "Count" because he seemed to be in the same league with the legendary composer and bandleader Duke Ellington. Basie's orchestra became famous for its smooth swing style. Some of the Count Basie Big Band hits were "One O'Clock Jump," and "Jumpin' at the Woodside."

FRANK SINATRA
SINGER AND ACTOR

BORN: *December 12, 1915, Hoboken*
DIED: *May 14, 1998, Los Angeles, CA*

Francis Albert Sinatra, the son of a New Jersey firefighter, won an amateur show in 1935. After that, he gained popularity singing with the "big bands" of Harry James and Tommy Dorsey. His solo career began on December 31, 1942. Soon huge crowds were mobbing him everywhere he went. In a sixty-year singing career, Sinatra made about 1,800 recordings and earned nine Grammy awards. Among his most famous recordings are "Luck be a Lady," and "My Way." Sinatra also had a successful acting career, winning an Academy Award for his role in *From Here to Eternity* (1953). He continued to perform until a few years before his death.

SARAH VAUGHAN
SINGER

BORN: *March 27, 1924, Newark*
DIED: *April 3, 1990, Hidden Hills, CA*

Sarah Lois Vaughan studied piano and organ as a child. Singing was her great talent, however, with a four-octave range stretching from soprano to

▲ **Frank Sinatra, famous vocalist.**

baritone. At eighteen, she won an amateur night contest at Harlem's famous Apollo Theatre and was soon working with jazz legends Billy Eckstine, Earl Hines, Charlie Parker, and Dizzy Gillespie. They created a jazz style known as bebop. As a solo singer, Vaughan earned the nickname "The Divine One." She became increasingly popular in the 1940s and 1950s with hits including "It's Magic," "Tenderly," and the million-selling "Broken-Hearted Melody." Vaughan continued her concert performances until shortly before her death in 1990.

ALLEN GINSBERG
POET

BORN: *June 3, 1926, Newark*
DIED: *April 5, 1997, New York, NY*

Allen Ginsberg is among the most influential poets of the late twentieth century. He was one of the main figures of the Beat movement, along with his friend Jack Kerouac. Ginsberg's first published work was *Howl and Other Poems,* in 1956. The first line of "Howl" is especially well-known: "I saw the best minds of my generation destroyed by madness..." Later works include "Kaddish" (1961), about the poet's relationship with his mother. Ginsberg was also a major influence on the hippie and counterculture movements of the 1960s.

JUDY BLUME
AUTHOR

BORN: *February 12, 1938, Elizabeth*

Best-selling author Judy Sussman Blume grew up in Elizabeth. She studied to be an elementary school teacher but found her true calling in writing. Blume has written books for all ages, from young children to adults. Her best-known works are probably those for young adolescents, especially *Are You There, God: It's Me, Margaret* and *Tales of a Fourth Grade Nothing*. Blume draws on her own childhood and uses New Jersey as the setting for many of her stories. Her readers appreciate Blume's willingness to explore real-life issues in her books. She has won more than ninety awards for her writing.

BRUCE SPRINGSTEEN
MUSICIAN

BORN: *September 23, 1949, Freehold*

Bruce Springsteen's career began with New Jersey bands. His first album with the E Street Band, in 1973, was *Greetings From Asbury Park, N.J.* It was a critical but not a commercial success. Springsteen's fame gradually increased with concert performances and the 1975 album *Born to Run*. The album *Born in the USA*, released in 1984, marked the peak of his popularity, selling more than twelve million copies. Other successful albums followed, along with an increasing focus on social causes. Springsteen — called "The Boss" — still occasionally shows up to play at a bar in Asbury Park called the Stone Pony.

New Jersey
History At-A-Glance

1524
Verrazano explores the New Jersey shore.

1609
Henry Hudson sails up what is now the Hudson River.

1638
Swedish settlers establish New Sweden in southern New Jersey.

1655
Swedes forced to give up New Sweden.

1664
New Netherland surrenders to England; colony granted to Berkeley and Carteret.

1673
Quakers buy West Jersey from Lord Berkeley.

1702
East and West Jersey united.

1746
Princeton University, originally the College of New Jersey, is chartered.

1766
Queen's College, today Rutgers University, is established.

1776
George Washington crosses the Delaware River to fight the Battle of Trenton.

1787
New Jersey becomes a state.

1790
Camden and Amboy Railroad line opens.

1600   **1700**   **1800**

1492
Christopher Columbus comes to New World.

1607
Capt. John Smith and three ships land on Virginia coast and start first English settlement in New World — Jamestown.

1754–63
French and Indian War.

1773
Boston Tea Party.

1776
Declaration of Independence adopted July 4.

1777
Articles of Confederation adopted by Continental Congress.

1787
U.S. Constitution written.

1812–14
War of 1812.

United States
History At-A-Glance

1811
The first U.S. ferry service runs between Hoboken and Manhattan.

1846
First recorded baseball game between two organized teams, the Knickerbockers and the New York Nine, in Hoboken.

1863
Draft riots occur in several New Jersey cities.

1878
John Holland builds the first viable submarine.

1896
The first professional basketball game is played in Trenton.

1912
Woodrow Wilson, the governor of New Jersey, is elected U.S. president.

1937
The *Hindenburg* crashes in Lakehurst.

1947
New Jersey's most recent constitution is adopted.

1962
Telstar 1 satellite, developed in New Jersey, is launched, transmitting live TV across the Atlantic.

1967
Riots in Newark kill twenty-six people.

1993
Christine Todd Whitman becomes the state's first woman governor.

1995
New Jersey Devils win their first Stanley Cup.

1800 — **1900** — **2000**

1848
Gold discovered in California draws 80,000 prospectors in the 1849 Gold Rush.

1861–65
Civil War.

1869
Transcontinental railroad completed.

1917–18
U.S. involvement in World War I.

1929
Stock market crash ushers in Great Depression.

1941–45
U.S. involvement in World War II.

1950–53
U.S. fights in the Korean War.

1964–73
U.S. involvement in Vietnam War.

2000
George W. Bush wins the closest presidential election in history.

2001
A terrorist attack in which four hijacked airliners crash into New York City's World Trade Center, the Pentagon, and farmland in western Pennsylvania leaves thousands dead or injured.

▼ A ZR3 zeppelin enters a hangar at the Naval Air Station in Lakehurst, circa 1924.

Festivals and Fun for All

Check web site for exact date and directions.

Cape May Hawk Watch, Cape May

Birding enthusiasts visit Cape May year-round, but every fall they come in droves to see the eighteen species of birds of prey that migrate through the area.

www.njaudubon.org/sites/hwcmbo.html

Chowderfest Weekend, Long Beach Island

Neither New England nor Manhattan has a lock on chowder. This seafood festival in October features fish and shellfish caught off the Jersey coast, but specializes in clam chowder. Everyone turns out for the Chowder Cook-Off Classic.

www.chowderfest.com

Christkindlmarkt, Stanhope

The colonial village of Waterloo is a National Historic Site offering tours and events year-round. Every December the village holds a *Christkindlmarkt*, or Christmas market, in the European holiday tradition.

www.waterloovillage.org

Good Ol' Days Festival, Manahawkin

Manahawkin Lake Park holds a railroad festival complete with historic reenactments and an evening concert.

www.discoversouthernocean.org/cofe/
calspecial.htm

Hambletonian Day, East Rutherford

The Hambletonian, one of harness racing's oldest and premier events, has been run at the Meadowlands every year since 1981.

www.hambletonian.org

Irish Fall Festival, North Wildwood

This four-day celebration of Irish culture includes dancing, music, a piper competition, and traditional crafts.

www.wildwoodbythesea.
com/irish

Miss America Week and Miss America Pageant, Atlantic City

The week prior to the crowning of Miss America in September is filled with celebrations amid the competitions.

www.missamerica.org

New Jersey Folk Festival, New Brunswick

For nearly thirty years undergraduates at Rutgers University have organized this free event, which features the diverse musical traditions found in the state of New Jersey. Crafts and foods are also part of the fun.

www.njfolkfest.rutgers.edu

▲ Harness racing is popular in New Jersey.

New Jersey Seafood Festival, Belmar

Named one of the top tourism events in New Jersey, the best of Jersey Shore seafood abounds at this June festival held on the shores of Silver Lake.
www.belmar.com/special/seafood.html

New Jersey State Fair/Sussex County Farm and Horse Show, Augusta

Everything from a woodchopping contest to an exhibit of baby farm animals is featured at this agricultural fair held in August. Many come just to see the horses, however. The Sussex County Horse Show is a weeklong event featuring nationally ranked competitions.
www.sussex-county-fair.org

Night in Venice, Ocean City

Decorated boats "parade" through Great Egg Harbor from Longport Bridge to Tennessee Avenue as Ocean City recreates the feel of Venice, Italy.
www.ocnjonline.com

QuickChek New Jersey Festival of Ballooning, Readington

More than 125 hot-air balloons make this the East Coast's largest balloon festival, but that's not all the fun that's in store. Vintage airplane exhibits, barnstorming demonstrations, live music, and fireworks provide nonstop entertainment.
www.balloonfestival.com/nj.html

Shad Fest, Lambertville

Pollution in the Delaware River killed off native fish populations in the 1970s, but today the river teems with aquatic life. The town of Lambertville celebrates the return of the shad each April with musical performances, arts and crafts, food, and the crowning of the Shad Queen.
www.lambertville.org/shad.html

Victorian Week, Cape May

Scenic Cape May is a seaside resort town that's also a National Historic Landmark famous for its wealth of Victorian buildings. Cape May residents relive a bygone era each year with a weeklong celebration of Victoriana.
www.capemay.to

▶ A Cape May house built in 1870.

Books

Armstrong, Harry and Tom Wilk. *New Jersey Firsts: The Famous, Infamous, and Quirky of the Garden State.* Philadelphia: Camino Books, 1999. For better or worse, New Jersey has often led the way.

Murray, Peter. *Perseverance! The Story of Thomas Alva Edison.* Plymouth, MN: The Children's World, Inc., 1997. Thomas Edison made some of the most important inventions in history while working in his New Jersey laboratories.

Peacock, Louise. *Crossing the Delaware: A History in Many Voices.* New York: Simon and Schuster, 1998. In 1776, George Washington and his men crossed the Delaware River to engage the British in the famous Battle of Trenton. This book tells the story of this event through excerpts of letters written by those involved in it.

Sherrow, Victoria. *The Hindenburg Disaster: Doomed Airship.* Berkeley Heights, NJ: Enslow, 2002. This book explores the possible causes of the Hindenburg disaster and describes what it was like to travel on the airship.

Stein, R. Conrad. *New Jersey.* New York: Children's Press, 1998. A book of information about the Garden State.

Web Sites

▶ Official state web site
www.state.nj.us
▶ Official Trenton web site
www.ci.trenton.nj.us
▶ New Jersey Historical Society web site
www.jerseyhistory.org

▶ New Jersey Department of Travel and Tourism web site
www.state.nj.us/travel

Note: Page numbers in *italics* refer to maps, illustrations, or photographs.